The Art of

Work

Jen Fitzgerald

D1608093

The Art of

Work

Jen Fitzgerald

Book Cover Design: Jeffrey Pethybridge
Book Interior Design: Sarah Gzemski

Cover photo credit: "The Last Strike" courtesy of the Joseph A. Labadie
Collection, University of Michigan.
Author photo credit: Thomas Sayers Ellis

Published by Noemi Press, Inc. A Nonprofit Literary Organization.
www.noemipress.org.

For the members of UFCW Local 342
in New York City, Labor Unions
across this world, and all who know
what work means, undocumented or not.

The Art of Work

The world would escape
to become all its never been
if only we would let it go
streaming toward a future without
purpose or voice.

Philip Levine

participatory
plutocracy

windows replaced
by the wind

begin
shattering

Mark Nowak
Shut Up Shut Down

Glossary of Terms

Product- Body manufactured
by social assimilation in turn

produces new product
of consumption for many fingered

consumer to consume. **Boss-**
The old guard needs coddling.

Who can ever work [for]
themselves? **Documented-**

exploitable force equal to
or less than the mass of a body

accelerated toward another body.
Body- the means of work, the unnegotiable

negotiable, our only barrier between
the soul and the world. **Bargaining-**

Show me yours and I'll stop
lying about mine. **Laboring Body-**

a symphony. **Labor Law-** to govern
the alleged inalienable- nothing

is implicit. **Worker's rights-**
workers righting the audacity

of necessity. **Undocumented-**
See "Documented."

Right to Strike-
As though permission

need be granted
to uncoil the body-

release from fangs
the venom of collective.

Battle Hymn: Generations

From mechanic to driver,
my grandfather never drifted
far from engines as movement,
engines as mechanism and his
hands grew rough with reverence.
Hands were the gears of his body.
As a child he dug in the mud
of Staten Island's marsh
for piss clams, proffered them
at restaurant back doors for candy
money. The Korean War drove
him to rub his teen-aged fingers
together as rack and pinion—
anxious shafts. Dodge-Chrysler
kept him employed in a system
of combustion that could be
contained. He would never drive
another make, never work in a shirt
without his name sewn in. He was
raised up by men like him, built up
his world with men like him
until it was safe to worry after
a time his hands might fail him.
In those later years, he ate lunch
with my grandmother, the matron
on his school bus. They returned
home, in step to learn one other
again. It would be quiet, splintered
until the day he could clear a space
for himself, line up tubes of
cadmium red, yellow ochre,
titanium white; line up mason jars
of turpentine to fill the nook with
a familiar chemical air. No matter
how many times he picked it up,

the frail body of the fan brush,
could not come comfortably
to rest between his calloused fingers
and palm creased with years
of creosote; black tributaries of time.
As a child, I sat alongside him
at the easel; fingers still, then suddenly
delicate strokes— a pine, a wave
breaking into smooth layers
of landscape. He clinked the brushes
in oil; the engine of his waking
mind at rest, rack and pinion
quaking in quiet creation. From
silence grew the smooth lull
of cylinders, the mindless memories,
both of us humming, *Roll the Union On*.

Last Totem of Tradesmanship

Take hands to aerial knife,
swipe, shoulder-slice tissue

as though there were
music behind it,

as though you were
keeping time.

Pull knife body down
the hung body,

ridging along ribs
to remove flank steak.

Marbled art carved from
a side of beef—

disconnect; reestablish
bond with flesh.

Talk to customers
as the last vestige

of language in this
linoleum way station.

But these people
are no constant;

a slideshow of flipped
faces on repeat.

Let the cut cow
of consciousness

drop— return
to meat room.

Pack out case,
stack Styrofoam trays—

their sheened cellophane,
glassine under

fluorescents. Hand under
hand, mounds of chopped

meat adorn themselves
in slick plastic. Line

them under window,
for customers to witness

our many-handed machine
of sustenance. We've all

been fed on the simplicity
of bread, meat, egg, and heat.

The meat room echoes
bleached air emptiness

in the slaps of hose on slick tile.
Run your finger along

the saw blade, an edge
like delicate lace.

Cutting boards at eye-level,
shift for light to run

like water across their surface.
You take pride in tools

of a trade that propel the human engine
forward. Hair-fine roots ground us

in the history of necessity;
hunt, fire, communion.

Replace the store's hat
with your Union hat

as New Guy checks
which train he'll catch.

Don't worry about the train,
From now on, I will drive you home.

You know about salary cuts,
store managers, about the bullshit

folks eat to stay fed.
You know about

throwing strike signs
at the gods of *have not*.

But patience is not taught—
it is lived as centuries wind

beams of time, as wisteria
vine blooms its brazen beauty.

Let youth learn lessons
of need, let it grab at the sun.

Redux

My brother stands at the block
chopping bone from flesh,
pulling flesh from sinew.

My brother stands for days,
shifting weight from ball to heel
in a dance he did throughout

his childhood— game controller
in hand, mouth taut in concentration;
he'd shed awareness of all other bodies

with the look of *elsewhere*—
the somewhere else in his eyes
making a machine out of maneuver.

My brother rocks himself
through an apprenticeship, with
the sway and steady of first steps,

pant cuffs reaching down and through
ground— the drilling of stance
and space to root his work in earth.

Sleepy Fishing Village at Sunrise

Splay the bodies as a gambler fans a flush;
dead pan clubs like fish eyes. Can't make it
to ten before the familiar tingle crawls
up your fingers. A false womb of frozen
salmon, shrimp, trout numbs your flesh
further. The glassine stare, dumb,
at something just above your shoulder.

Waves like people will crash your small
corner, carting body heat, bringing
solid and scaled to a discerning nose.
Analog counterweight clacks against
the chain as they double weigh—
in New York City, we know better
than to trust the wares we are handed.

Manager was your *buddy*, till Workman's Comp
denied small claim on your own pay.
You can't help but test rubber grips
against your thumbnail—
fear the depth, the spill that kept you
on your back for weeks. Engine kicks cold
air down on your wares, your back.

The product must be kept cold, employees kept colder—
when they thaw, they speak, notice long hours
stretched and dragged like Clydesdale-labor.

Electronic doors open to wind warm breeze
down clutter of end caps. The salted air
of Coney Island grazes your cheek
like the marina mist of a fishing boat
pulling free of Mill Basin. The international
water hums its own pollination, grabbing
seed and scent from every curve of the earth.

I Hear a Voice Calling From On High

From "Bow Down" come "Rise Up,"
Come they Lion from the reeds of shovels,
The grained arm that pulls the hands,
They Lion grow.

Philip Levine

The hymn and grate of Union Hall
buzzes a catechism of contract.

Collective bargaining [of bread and body]
is nothing less than a sea swelling

and launching an arm of wave
at the shore. Company needs

to be called out on a chorus
of bullshit. [Raise a fist, an Amen]

They want to drop seniority,
create a part time army

of pseudo workers, with a severance
that couldn't keep cats fed.

Union Officers guide a collective
of willing. There will be no

hat-in-hand office visit,
no *head-on-stake* sacrifice.

[Be the gods they appease]
Now stand and Vote—

motherfuckers
are about to listen up.

Survival: Generations

1

I've watched my grandmother pull potatoes
from a pot of boiling water. I've watched

the detachment of a woman who's scoured
floors with caustic powder for 45 years,

of a woman who's buried her boy.
I've flinched at my grandmother's muscular

hands scrubbing my skin as though
it adhered to my bones by grout.

We may be poor, but we're clean.

2

She saves and keeps— terrified of waste,
and need. She adapts and tailors folklore,

writes herself in to the stories I will tell
my daughter— about *Ralphie*, the orphaned

opossum near death in front of the house,
huddled near his cooling mother. He lived

in the hood of her sweatshirt as a pouch.
I will tell her about the litter of newborn

mice found nested my sweater, how she
nursed them with an eye dropper of tuna water

until each died and was buried.
I know they're rodents, but they're living things.

Suffering: the amorphous, ever-present nameless.

3

When I teach my daughter what it means
to become a woman I want her to picture

mixing milk and ground meal in her palm
for baby birds. When I teach her what it means

to be a woman, I want her to think of a body
hell-bent on keeping life, of knowing the beating

ache of creation. When I teach my daughter
what it means to have been a woman,

I want her to see the small, black nose
peeking out of my grandmother's hood

as she stitched a hem.

Survey of Silt

Your body: a dash on a graph,
delineated by passing
unconscious ticks.

1.9 hours daily bread and water.

A puddle measures its life in raindrops;
2 billion before it's called back to the sky.

1.37 hours on weekends and holidays.

Time management dissected
like a paralyzed sparrow.

Religious
obligations grow
by .03 hours,
Sunday

when planes mimic V's of migration
for fuel efficiency— mechanical arms extend
featherless and southward.

      4.73 leisure hours a day.

Volleyball injuries are
serving up, spiking down,
serving up, spiking down,
pounding air with delicate
rivets of friction.

1.9% Productivity increase
coupled with labored
breathing cost decrease of 1%

slows down the line,
move over to the side
if you plan to die.

And 4,609 will—
458 by homicide;

Of the 1,800 images in a single minute
of stop animation, only one frame
will burn itself off the reel—
jump to its death over
the whip of projector slap.

Line-mate, wrench;
adulterer, blade.

All murderer and murdered—
loves we molt to slice our pie
chart of a life have

to fall somewhere- sweep them up,
convince your country
you wouldn't kill for a job.

Pebble Ripples the Surface

Ducks trample for crumbled
bread; save crumbs for stoic

decoy at pond's center.
Ask them: into whose gaping

mouth do you toss bits of food?
Hand to mouth: Universal

gesture for *my hunger*
is of no consequence.

I marched across the street,
fists heavy with coin
we'd scavenged from around
the house and counted twice

on kitchen counter. Deli Man
won't rip *us* off. If the price
stayed true to the cent,
the gallon went next

to the register, next to my pile
of coin. In this lesson
I am seven
and have to stand still

as Deli Man counts nickels
and pennies. I puff out in display.
In this lesson, the milk
is for my brothers' bottles

so I look him in the eye
and hold my breath
till he opens the cash
drawer and overfills the tray.

My family's version of survival
is insular. The best defense is mistrust—
of neighbor, of cousin, of stranger,
your own breath betraying weakness.

The Killing Floor is Slick

Captive bolt pistol hacks, hisses,
      heaves cow to the floor.
            Hook the hooves— invert bodies;

suits on a dry cleaner's
      motorized line. Purple veins
            scarlet muscle. A single

slice, skin folds back
      like theatre curtains. Parse
            mammoth down to salable

in minutes. Whir of buzz saw, clack
      of cleaver. Move fatal air
            through piston, a gear's precision;

a machine, you are— single file
      death march, zapped
            forward by arcs of electricity.

Lost count now, thought it foolish
      to keep tally after 20 years.
            Men never talk about wide

bovine eyes drifting through dreams,
      flashing past tender moments
            when your little one flits her lashes

against yours. Time trudges,
      Novocaine dripped through a dull
            syringe, numbing nothing.

The Bridge Keeper

1

My father used the string
of Christmas lights as an easy
example of a series circuit.
If one bulb is cut off, subsequent

bulbs are extinguished. The more
you add, the more go dim, tax
the source. But what of those
first few meters of amperes,

what of those survivors? If my family
were a circuit we would be parallel—
my father would be the tripping
fuse, the fracture on the breaker,

the step down transformer.

2

In this creation myth, the gods are
sociopaths— they teach us to love
them as they love themselves. In this
creation myth, the gods made my

father to bring sun over the Atlantic's
black horizon— made him so undeniably
human that his ascension over cables
and arches would bring him no closer

to their feet, no closer to the rumored
flight of glory. My father designed
the lighting sequences by which our
bridges greet the night. Through

the god's creation, New York City
comes alight. Now, he hangs himself
over the harbor in gloaming, tender
to the bulbs of our insomnia.

In suspension, he connects centuries
to evenings. In tethered flight,
he conducts control from the source.
He is the source.

We are a family of creators, of bridges—
we form passageways. Energy can be
neither created nor destroyed, it moves
in arcs from body to body. With every

swipe of the hand, black-blinding rage
was transferred to me. With every swipe
of the tongue, generations of fear heaved
anxious breaths in my chest. I carry

the charged metallic dust of inheritance.

3

My second Great Grandfather walked
the Brooklyn Bridge the day it opened,
the day he came from Berlin, the day
he decided Brooklyn held more promise

than the Black Forest and death drum
of war world, take one. A wave of
immigration from Germany, cresting
after the previous wave and waning

for the next— a succession of political-
refugee-religious-soldiers-of-there
must be a way to own oneself.
He marched through revelry, baptized

us by fire into this transient society.
Forty-six years to the day, that bridge
bore my grandfather into this world.
On her 125th year, after year and child

and motherless and year, death, drink,
and restless year, she snatched him back out.
[Dear Reader, if any of this be lies, strike
me dead here, in this sunlit square foot.]

The bridge has borne the weight of our shame.

4

This family doesn't have girls,
makes only great men with engineer
minds who measure time by tension
and compression. How much pull

will fracture, how much push
will fissure? My father trusses
himself in the gap of his past
and does not see what expanse

lay beyond time's horizon. But our
Berlin forbearer, walked that span
to bear witness to my creation myth—
I am the copper wire that jumps

current, the body that grabs at bulbs.
I hold an unwitting light to generations'
blackness, of children kept in closets
and cruelty like mallets— down, down,

brought down, and again in the form
of father, of sister, in the form of mother,
of self. We learn quickly that ancestry squats
in the body, malignant and invisible.

I am the insulator of these unforgivable truths.

5

When the conductor came home
he shed his rubber soles, scrubbed
the heavy metals from his arms.
It may have been days—his absence

hung like a forgotten shirt in the stale
closet of our hours. He was always
at work until the idea of being *at work*
became lost in routine. He rested

his plastic tea mug on the edge
of the couch. My brothers and I
would watch him, poised or primed,
and have no idea who he was.

We never understood the charge
behind our initial flash— so we sat
quietly; each load powered
independently from the source;

each load flickering beside him.

Here is the Life We've Made For You

1

Leather belt strapped.
Plastic helmet, plastic glasses;

Holster filled with sharpened blades.
Meat hangs, menacing on hooks—

stacked like pine trees
        branches splayed.

Floor manager seethes
behind skinned flesh.
in thick, meat room air,
earthy blood.

Cut, scrape, move to the left.
Cut, scrape, move to the left.
Bone fragments fleck
off protective glasses.

Cut, scrape, move to the left.
Had it out for you since
your daughter got sick.

Repeat swerves,
sleights of hand.
Cut, scrape, move to the left.

Union told him to *fuck off*,
you've got a contract.

2

That smell is blood,
connective tissue slapped on the floor,
primal fluid,
your pulse raised like a teaspoon of adrenaline,
fades

but instinct lingers
like the fat clogging
your sole's gaps- scrape
your boots down the edge
of a wooden pallet.

Retreat to the splintered
picnic table to breathe
dead air; eat a sandwich.

Hunt's Point Meat Market
is a series of loading bays,
box trucks, and dumpsters
where bees swarm the sun-cooked
concrete.
Breathe in the sweet smell of rot—
it's blue collar,
it's a trade,
        it'll feed your kids.

Small bee leaves the swarm,
lands on your flesh-specked arm.
Do not swat it.

Let it rest on the lingering death
between your two bodies;
decide where it ends
and you begin.

3

Trim the fat, pass,
repeat.

Cutting room is abuzz;
32 white coats
manning machines,
passing pieces down.

There were 55 when you started.
Less arms to cut,
more bodies to cut up.

14 cleavers hack at bone,
20 jigsaw blades beat
the clasps as a feral cat
rattling its trap.

Pails of bloodied femurs
and plastic containers stacked,
filled with indiscernible debris.

Tension still squats,
from the walk-out
turned lock-out.

Workers disabled
their machines,
Workers, their words like fists.
Benefit cuts.

Return to the smell,
you can't get away
from the slick smell
of snakes mating
in your gut.

[Human Resource Handbook Section 7, Part B: It is best to inform
an employee of their termination on a Friday. They will then
have Saturday and Sunday to process their emotions without
a reasonable chance for retaliation and a succession of Mondays
with which to internalize and self-deprecate. Convince them
to forfeit sick days, vacations, and their right to unemployment.]

4

Warehouse, wholesale-
behind-the-scenes.

Filet Mignon, Rib-eye, Halal.

Second chancers- once lifers
paroled to the trade.

Porterhouse, Short Ribs, Kosher

Work release- released from work
to tainted air.

Stew meat packed, shipped by truck.

                    Cigarette hangs from his mouth
                    as he signs for cargo, drives off.

5

Mike grips the corona bottle
like a scraper, flexes each finger
out in a scythe curve-
teaching them how
to ease up after a shift.

Jose mixes languages
like a slurry of chopped meat,
La cuchilla almost got me
again today. Eases into
the splintered picnic table.

When you close your eyes,
remind your hunched shoulders
to release like wings stretching,
shaking out the hard won roost.
It is easy to love these men;

the ones with warrants,
the ones with
old ladies chomping
at the bit
back home.

6

Wash your hands
after changing.
Industrial strength soap
can't lift the stench,
can't fill the cracks

fissuring their way
around your palms.
Blisters sting
like wasps of slaughter.

Twist fare over and around
your fingers as you
head to the bus.
Remove the chain
hanging your

scratched ID.
The third grade picture
sitting behind it
as though you could
just flip around, hold her—

always asleep
when you get home.
Bus driver pulls lever,
releases door, nods
and drives off.

The Singing Polar Bear

One

Breaking now,
means hauling
overnight; flat
roof sleeper

like coffin.
Twilight
till no light,
nothing sits still.

Tussled sheets,
strewn movies-
cab feels lived in.

Miles like hours
or mountains to bridges
past busses in tunnels.

*

Blew two retreads
on last haul-
threw to I 80
Gator Graveyard.

Mental tally
clicks subconscious
ticker, deducts-
only deducts.

Rag-tag home
stretched across states-
sofa sits in Iowa,
feet reclined in Ohio.

Pottsville
to Williamsburg
to Fallsburg
and again.

*

Hum of reefer body
soothes, not brays
like livestock trailer,
heaving its weight

against turns,
rocking each
other to calm
in the womb
of a cramped trailer.

Drop off sides
of beef,
butchered meat,
for live cows;
Lazarus of the road.

Blue

    Work for   live for
    work
    life   living for work
    working life living
    for life work
    a life's work
    like it's life

a population
evicted from history

tunneling New York City
only one of many laborers,
only a many of one laborer
eyes squinting at the camera's flash
down the shaft

a history of eviction
Lower East to the Island
or in this case, Staten Island

surfing landlords

riddled
with rickets   *Shanty Irish*

well-worn term of endearment
or
text book
     trauma

so old it's in black and white
so ingrained
that it's
passed on in the genes

to kids

who still their voices still
when phantom landlords
bang on the door

       so far
       we haven't come
       from this
       yet, so far haven't we
       how far,
       have we come from this—
       not yet.
       haven't we
       come so far?
       yet,
       we have come from this.

Diner Waitress

One

Five AM fire up the flat top; crack six dozen eggs for omelets and scratch a trill of whisk on bowl; staggered waitress shifts put three on the floor till lunch; singing a breakfast language of steam and burnt fingers, passed down— twenty-one *Over Well, burn the hash*, an oral lineage of women seeing men off to work— *thirty-one, scrambled easy on the pot; all of it on legs if you're not in the weeds*; denying their own seeing as working; every seat is full for the breakfast rush and circus act of cups and saucers stacked four high; tables turn over two at a time; bussers unstick dollar bills from syrup rings, under a constant smell of bacon; the rush of a push wears off when you finally sit— feel your calves throb a satisfying ache; we were in the business of favors—turning over tables for a crapshoot salary; women who work for whims with sensible shoes and a fake grin; knowing nothing; could be more American; than an unsure future—

Two

I was invincible because I could *earn*; hadn't I shredded the walls of this myth?; *only earning* is a community college sort of invisible; even if here is better than dead, stop letting me in; pulling doubles at a local spot; couldn't put your plates in the slop without dishwasher going for a grab; seasoned waitresses perfected harmlessness; or conceded to a fallacy of flattery; rat on a busser and forget your tips; rat on a man to a manager and become the bitch pariah of the diner; had my run in; boss put me on notice; gripped my arm and pulled me in; a red hand imprint for hours; how much of this body was mine; dishwasher watched; I angled my torso at the sink to lay plates and hightail it out; but he got me— pinched my breast over shirt; made contact with a piece of me I don't want back, blackened; and what of shock; and what of red-faced rage; what of futility reborn as action; I pulled a steak knife out of a slop bucket; aimed it at his beating wreck; *touch me again and I gut you like fish motherfucker*; he laughed; there is no power here; that which he enacts on me is enacted on him; a woman willing to stand on her feet for fourteen hours can't have sharpened edges; he steals from me what has been stolen from him; entitled; a body; in that kitchen, a body; the men came in and I couldn't take a joke; a body; lighten up; in that kitchen, something must be sharp; the knives would never cut deep enough for my muscles to unclench.

Three

My shift is almost over; heaved a mountain again; all that exertion for inches, for grabs at nothing; fake ass Sisyphus; another waitress gone today; she fought back; sent to walk the diner stroll for a few laps; it's all build up; when we reach the apex we're cliff-side, closed eyes; the march of this life is supposed to be straight— A to B; birth to death; but the cycle dips out in the middle; trips up and back around; I told him I quit; he told me I'll be back; I may believe him; through the one-sided window, I see the pollen has fallen from the flowering trees, coating everything in pallid yellow; it must be Spring; dusted cars back out of parking spaces; drive out of view; a browning dish rag hangs limply from my apron; I pull it off; all is shattered, somehow clean.

Seeker's Hymnal

Who heralds the many,
reflected on pages,

hears the chirps
of winter migration-

All toil, all life.

From seedling to sproutling,
from dead tree to felled tree,

we build our defenses
against death's natural menace.

All life, all toil.

Seekers sing at the finding
but knowing is quiet

when there's nothing left
to listen for.

Processing Plant, So. Fallsburg, N.Y.

1

Perpetually a few shudders
from ecstasy,

the building vibrates its death
in puffs

of pulverized bone and undercoat.
Beneath

overhang out from rain, workers
blow smoke

at tiny feathers surfing air. Shuffling
in galoshes,

cowl-eyed, they move from locker
to glove,

to knife; ankle grab at conveyor
belt of fluttering.

Kosher Law neck slitting, draining—
then flood

break room, squeeze into too
few tables.

Behold the mechanism that feeds
the blade,

throats. By noon, thin pink fills
blood room.

2

Migrant, immigrant, emigrated-
boot cover

hooves clomp moist cement.
USDA

countdown of freshness punctuates
shifts by stages

of decay, flicks worker ears in native
tongue.

Dress yourself, feed machine, breathe,
eat, dress

poultry, breathe, divvy down to wing
and breast,

breathe, wrap in cellophane. *10,000
chickens*;

overseers set watches to sundown.
300 workers

keep unconscious calendars, know
Holy Shabbat

by vacancy. *24 hours*. Goliath must not,
I repeat, must not rest.

3

Dressed trucks, live trucks line the lot.
Plastic pallet

stacked chickens jockey for an inhale,
flinch

at fileted breasts passing their periphery.
One spare

feathered baby slips free from ankle
clasps, pecks

at her own massacre, hosed down,
down the drain.

The Singing Polar Bear

Two

Wall of bobtails
flanks diesel
pumps; drivers
stretch out to pay

showers, chewing
tobacco, to feel
legs again. It's not
about food, but heat

filling your belly
and a truck stop
waitress that smiles
like your wife.

Caffeine, AM, FM,
taurine, CB, satellite;
without hubodometer
and the chicken coop
you'd never stop.

*

Night haulers call you
The Singing Polar Bear—

a special call sign
for when pitch ticks

over to dawn—
a distant dream

of history in a
lit life of scenery.

Dark hour roadsides
turn into cadavers

of anxious possibility
Your voice fills the empty,

and I hear you cousin—
shooting skip over

the ionosphere,
singing Hank Williams

to the disembodied
many, eyes fixed ahead.

Bargaining

The Ask: Employees may never fall ill.
The Get: Workers beg, barter, beat bodies
out of sick. The Ask: Never an injury
on the line. The Get: Workmen's comp
shattered like porcelain; broken bones
and limps hidden. The Ask: Four children
to lock in desperation; they may never fall
ill. The Get: Who-comes-in-where blame
game- cook little brother breakfast, don't
wake them, anger them. The Ask: We just
want quiet, a labor force of yes, American
Dream, day dream, dream a little dream,
old time religion, don't stop believing,
muscle, sports, madness, spit shined, moon
shined, good-natured consent. The Get: This.

The Hinge on Which We Turn

The mass
a mass   body
a wave
fat stroke of red
over a blur of brown
dotted, dotted, dotted
with white
amorphous translucent
and then movement
and then swirling
and then striking

Paint anger like fire—
Those bosses are gonna

make them pay   Those bosses
like to bash their bossiness
all over the God Damned world

        press the pen down
        this started with a vote

press the pen down
to leach the ink

        What begins in the wrist
        ends in the fist

An ecstasy of possibility bursts
from back room to street.

The lines are drawn in.
I see an arm now;

a shoe and another,
        beating concrete flat, flat,

        steps to hell
        where the dead bang

ceilings with brooms.
        A series of long strokes for

parade barricades
blue-collar side show;

or sand bar heaving shoulders
against incoming waves.

Pencil in police now
to brood between

        store and strike and line.
        In this marching

        it doesn't matter
        who'll lunge first.

Now draw in a mouth—
Aint you in a Union too?

An image offers no back story
leave that to history.

Hot air rat arrives, filled
like Councilwoman

            at the camera. Off the page
            and on to the reel— bilingual

mic check— constituent
count off. Scabs dressed

in white, crossing a line,
scabs picking at their own

sanitized flesh,
crossing a shift in means.

            The Union can't feed you forever.
            No one promised to take care of you.

We are tired of inaction,
weary of the pulpit.

Bodies are cut from
the crowd as though

severing is shoring up.
        Where is the fight taken down to dirt?

Where is solidarity
        when it requires only empathy?

This circle is worn down from your walking
and in my waking I see you—

I see us honking, waving,
writing songs about your

sanctioned raging. But we
diverge, pretend to starve for our art,

when this march, this labor,
this fear, this time of simplifying

begs of us strokes—
to be drawn in thicker,

sturdier;
to be drawn in fully

and remembered as something
that once stood on its own.

Egg Factory, Thompsonville, N.Y.

Prepare for a storm each day,
wish you could dress in a slick jacket,
galoshes, and some polymer that resists

the sludge you wade through.
Once menacing factory now makes landscape
limp. Workers push through enormous doors

into the building-like hanger. What bastard
birth created such drudgery?
Stagnant gray hits the walls, splatters

to inhabit the in between air. Sick green,
blackened coffee, faded blue, a cacophony
of stimuli- ground yourself;

there are only primary colors; three.

An agony of bright bursts through slits
in corrugated tin, refracted
by the repetitive hum of an industrial fan

banging seconds like jail cell tallies.
The chickens move severely.
Necks jerk in pecking seizure,

tilting acknowledgment. You named
them when things needed names. But now
you are these tools: shoveled arms,

pails as hands, rake teeth, sharpened.
Adjust useless paper mask; it soaks
up stench, holds it to your nose on a rusted platter.

Town complains of yellowed
sulfur air, rivers thick with effluent.
They don't care that each breath

drowns anew. EPA dips sticks
in river, factory fined. No government
agency tests blood for sediment.

Cage on cage; hens like mausoleums.
You know what it's like, women
piled ten high, avian pox blubbling

white and yolk across hands.
Union Organizers squeeze through
membership cards. Write in: Name,

Job Title, Rate of Pay. The second
time Boss smiled at you, an envelope
for y*our cooperation during*

the union election. You left it
on his desk at the end of shift.
The first time he smiled at you,

hands down your shirt, clawing.

Boss' shadow distorts constant downpour
of feathers; feathers in your hair,
on your lip, in your socks. An angel

rain of plumes like gathered corn silk.

Forage eggs from cages,
shoulder them to sorting room.
Mechanical movements

drag by hours of tossing
cracked and oozing.
Discolored shipped to plants

for manipulation; liquefied,
powdered. Be grateful you don't
work where powdered egg

puffs in ominous clouds, seeks
sponge of lungs. Retail only
wants perfectly shaped, bleached,

shined eggs split in twelves
to stock their shelves.
Sort your last basket, twenty

minutes till you can shower-
scrape off the day. Egg in front
of you draws your eye down;

wobbles. A delicate crack
and shift, opening a slit.
An impossible, slime-coated

wing testing air, stretches out.

My Mother Never Smoked A Cigarette

My mother's cough breaks silences. My mother's
cough creates silences. Her lungs bellow the smoke
of felled buildings in hair-fine moments of moving

air between hacking; dilation of tissue absorbing
what it can. Her children sift through walled
off memories as she sifted through remnants on

September 12th, 13th, 14th... Conveyer belt of pieces;
separate the organic from inorganic. What they meant
was, find chunks big enough to mail to bereaved

families. This is your job; what the NYPD expects.
Wear this gauge at your chest, it will beep when
the air can be wrung out, dripping toxic sludge.

Bring your team to higher ground until next round
of dust settles. What you don't breathe you absorb;
become many. Are you ready to walk sediment

of the fallen through this life? She refused the doctor,
knew he would scope her lungs and call out, *concrete,*
rebar, soda can, train track, toe. Picture her

knee deep, waist deep, neck deep; tugging, gasping;
bussed over the Verrazano bridge, carted
to Staten Island dump in hazmat suit.

A finger, an atom set aside for identification.
Suspire the expired, hold them in until
your lungs scream in pathetic wheezes.

We all breathed death that day. For some, its chest still
rises and falls, makes my mother's lungs whistle as an
asthmatic choir. Single moment in St. Paul's Chapel,

the unbreakable church, stained glass impervious
to the trembling colossi. *This is where they brought us
for a break, a bottle of water. It was always so quiet.*

Her children can't release her from memories.
She will forever pull herself from the pew
and walk toward the dust of hell, rasping.

The Art of Work

To photograph is to frame.
To frame is to exclude.
                        Susan Sontag

If they call them Garden Apartments,
you'll smell a suggested spring,

not insidious-mold-weighed walls
and lead paint. This assembly line

community of garnished wages
and ethnic divisions muddles what is

constructed and what is "God-given."
Boss offers you transport to the plant,

so you'll forget they've dropped you
in someone else's yard, face-first.

Those someones are up in arms
about you coming into their yard.

[Civilized peoples do not have
sweatshops within eye-shot]

Those someones think
they'll feed themselves.

What do you dream
in *Beverly Gardens,*

with the feral cats,
burnt out washroom,

purgatory of a town?
Maybe just grateful.

[what they've done to
you makes them ugly, ugly, not you]

Maybe spreading
seed for song birds,

planting sunflowers
to defy gravity—

stand taller
than children

hoisting one another
up for petals.

We came for you,
        we two recorders.

In our images
you pose a weekday,
        you pose a workday
to make artifice of living.

        The roll advances one grab forward.

The art of my work
is the lens change;
switch out, retreat.

                Don't think less of me
                because I wept after we left
                the chicken plant—
                think less of me because
                I am telling you.

The art of your work
is the frozen permeable,
the captured frame—

                Image makers of witness
                mean to be seen
                in your portrait.

[veins are mapped
as a river inlet, outlet
to the beating
that keeps us both alive]

All of us
are in the position
to be consumed.

Hudson Valley

By the time leaves hit ground,
they are muddied and mute. Autumn

soil sinks as you trail behind yourself
on the short trek from worker housing

to the pens. Midnight feeding, 3 AM, 6 AM.
Only varied light punctuates your shifts.

Ducks dart, beak for grain in the dirt
as you approach. Pull the mechanical arm

from its high perch, jam the tiny shovel
deep down the duck's throat. Esophagus

dilates, corn pours in. Small body
stocks for long digestion down lines

of longitude to Mississippi
Aullurial Valley. You've heard the liver

grows from sickness, alcohol; wonder if
it feels like a fetus pressing its heel

out in a stretch. You've never tasted foie gras.

Ducks gather in make-shift ponds,
turn their gaze upward to watch

kin's V's making the instinctual
journey- floating through chilled

stellar map. You all drifted here;
axes of polarized light. Migration

of species meet in feeder and food-
slid to drudgery under Jim Crow,

to a bed in third class, as in: citizen,
as in: no union for you. Boss deducts

for housing, deducts for protective
gear, for the two dead ducks.

Your mother in Honduras,
think of her, of the man

who cloaked you, pulled you
over the border. Think of

the eight years you've lived
with water fowl, toiled over

a tiny organ; bloated, extracted,
seared, served. It was a Monday

when his furious gait bounded
the feeding floor. Straightened,

did not rise. Other workers
at lunch. Either food or antibiotics

in the bare cabinets of
mandatory worker-housing.

Bodies take what they need
to survive, nourishment drug

from the bones and teeth
to pump the heart— bodies take

what they want when the taking
feeds the feral, the bleating quiet.

Broken Spanish raises the hair
on your neck. Hands untainted

by rough splintered farm tools,
pulled you down in a thud,

a dry earth-coated ceremony.
You could not cry out, finger flesh

pushing down on your bared teeth.
Ducks struggled back

in anxious waves,
monotone chorus of quacking

drowned out his grunting,
your gasping

under dead weight.
Remember picking

hay, cracked corn
from your hair for hours—

the fence stretching
up at impossible angles,

heeled grooves in the dirt
outliving three rainstorms.

Close your eyes.

When you open them,

shove this back
into the recesses,

buried under the pens
and harried ducks.

But it lingers like hunger.
Lingers because he resurrects

every day in you,
every time you nurse his son.

Afterword/Onward

For all its
sordid spinning,
this world
has always
been yours.

From the felled
tree [unite] sprouts
a seed starting
just [resist]a little
higher, clawing
its way [rise up]
to the sun.

Notes on Collaborative Labor:

I will not pretend that these poems were born in a vacuum.
Everything in this collection is lived experience: mine, my family's,
Thomas Sayers Ellis, Members of UFCW Local 342, and the
undocumented agricultural workers unable to organize.

If I am to have compassion, I do not get to meter it out. Compassion
for the workers, the victims, the victimizers, the viewers, the image
makers, and all the bodies taking up space in between.

> Collaboration—to sever after the fact, is a lie.

The poems of my working class and my family's working class
histories and realities were born of difficulty. I worked to honestly
render these experiences into art, to elevate them to the level at which
they deserved to be lifted. This book, quite literally struggled to make
it into your hands. It is from this struggle that I have grown as an
artist. It is for overcoming this struggle that I am filled with gratitude.

But my gratitude does not blind me to the reality of exploitation.
Those of us who are preyed upon for perceived weakness must band
together so that nothing can be taken that we did not wish to give.
Our strength and power in this union is undeniable, unimpeachable,
and unstoppable.

Acknowledgments:

Thank you to the journals who featured these poems:

Eckleburg Review: Survey of Silt, My Mother Never Smoked a Cigarette
Harriet: The Poetry Foundation Blog: Processing Plant: So. Fallsburg, NY
and portions of earlier poems
PEN Anthology: The Killing Floor Is Slick
Political Punch Anthology: My Mother Never Smoked a Cigarette
THEThe Poetry Blog's Infoxicated Corner: I Hear A Voice Calling From On High,
Survival: Generations

Thank you to Carmen Gimenez-Smith for rising to the many needs of this text, its author, and the literary community. And to Sarah Gzemski for your help, guidance, and vision. You both helped me realize a collection far beyond what I had imagined.

Thank you to my early eyes on these pieces, my poetry family, my literary community, my class-warriors, and all of you doing the good work.

Thank you to the members of UFCW Local 342 for letting me in to your job sites as an observer, for your patience, your kindness, and for showing me how the term "bad ass" could be taken to an entirely new level.

Thank you to laborers, Union members, Union Administrators, and the seen and unseen of our working world. Thank you for everything you do to lift one another up, create the collective, and keep the global wheels turning.

And thank you to Thomas Sayers Ellis, who lived these poems with me, who taught me how to locate the image-maker in me, nurtured it, and showed me I had the right to be creative, to make art of work and life.

Jen Fitzgerald is a poet, essayist, community activist, and a native New Yorker who received her MFA in Poetry at Lesley University. She is the host of New Books in Poetry Podcast, a member of New York Writers Workshop, and curates the Annapolis reading series "Poets in the Garden." She teaches "Writing the Silence," a workshop she created to help writers interrogate the synaptic leaps in their work. Her work has been featured on PBS Newshour and Harriet: The Poetry Foundation Blog and in Tin House, Salon, PEN Anthology, among others. She is now in the D.C. area and at work on her memoir.